A Crabtree Roots Book

Un libro de Las Raíces de Crabtree

FARM ANIMAL FRIENDS

Animales de granja amistosos

SHEEP
OVEJAS

AMY CULLIFORD

SANTIAGO OCHOA

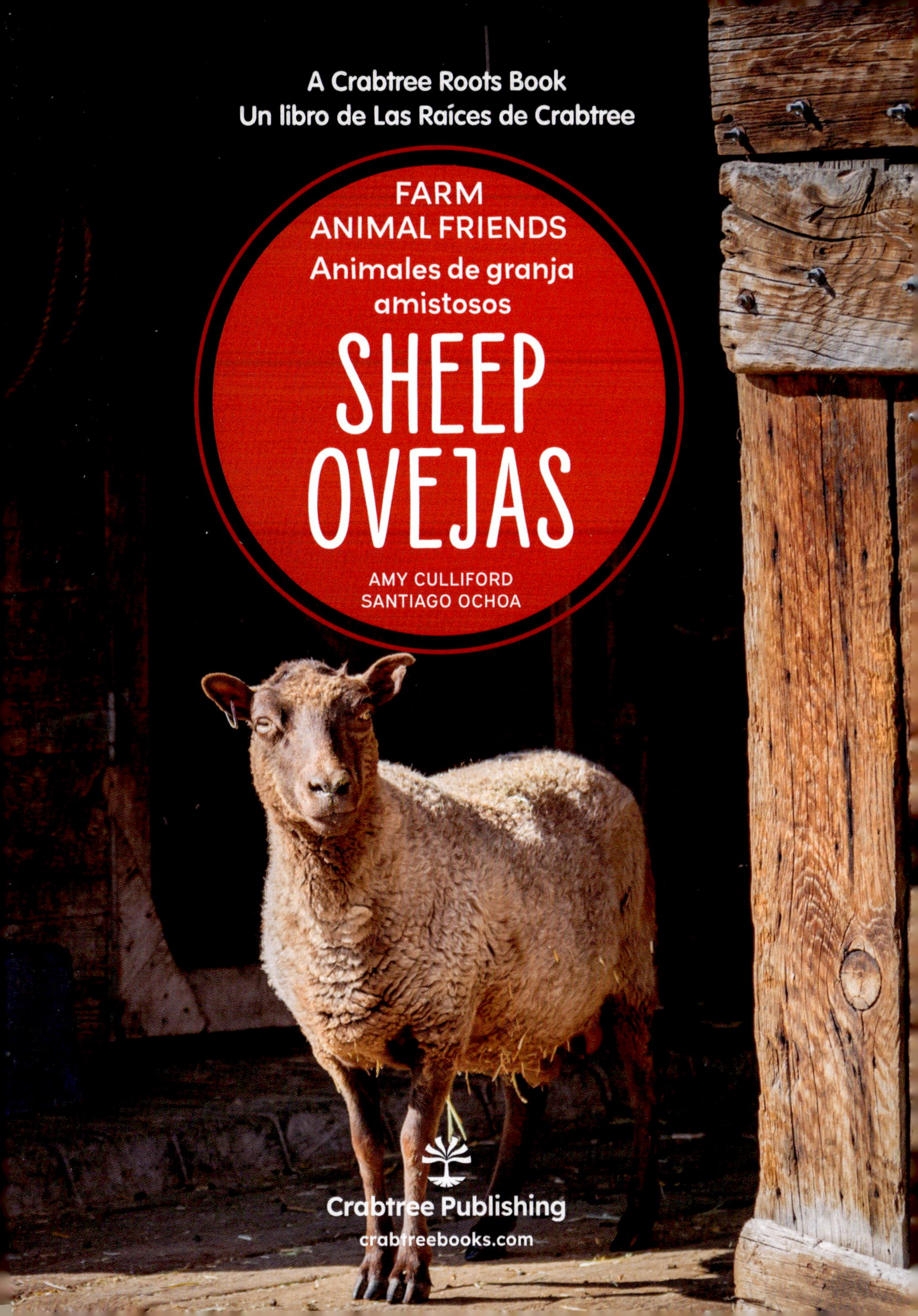

Crabtree Publishing

crabtreebooks.com

School-to-Home Support for Caregivers and Teachers

This book helps children grow by letting them practice reading. Here are a few guiding questions to help the reader with building his or her comprehension skills. Possible answers appear here in red.

Before Reading:

- What do I think this book is about?
    - *This book is about sheep.*
    - *This book is about sheep on farms.*

- What do I want to learn about this topic?
    - *I want to learn what sound a sheep makes.*
    - *I want to learn what colors sheep can be.*

During Reading:

- I wonder why...
    - *I wonder why some sheep are different colors.*
    - *I wonder why some sheep have horns.*

- What have I learned so far?
    - *I have learned that sheep live on farms.*
    - *I have learned that sheep can be big or little.*

After Reading:

- What details did I learn about this topic?
    - *I have learned that some sheep have horns.*
    - *I have learned that sheep can be different colors.*

- Read the book again and look for the vocabulary words.
    - *I see the word* ***farm*** *on page 5 and the word* ***horns*** *on page 12. The other vocabulary words are found on page 14.*

This is a **sheep**.

Esta es una **oveja**.

These sheep are on a **farm**.

Estas ovejas están en una **granja**.

Some sheep are big.

Algunas ovejas son grandes.

Some sheep are little.

Algunas ovejas son pequeñas.

Sheep can be white, brown, or black.

Las ovejas pueden ser blancas, cafés o negras.

Some sheep have **horns**.

Algunas ovejas tienen **cuernos**.

All sheep say, *baa*!

Todas las ovejas dicen
¡bee!

Words to Know
Palabras para aprender

farm
granja

horns
cuernos

sheep
oveja

33 Words

This is a **sheep**.

These sheep are on a **farm**.

Some sheep are big.

Some sheep are little.

Sheep can be white, brown, or black.

Some sheep have **horns**.

All sheep say, *baa*!

35 palabras

Esta es una **oveja**.

Estas ovejas están en una **granja.**

Algunas ovejas son grandes.

Algunas ovejas son pequeñas.

Las ovejas pueden ser blancas, cafés o negras.

Algunas ovejas tienen **cuernos**.

Todas las ovejas dicen *¡bee!*

FARM ANIMAL FRIENDS
Animales de granja amistosos

SHEEP
OVEJAS

Crabtree Publishing

crabtreebooks.com 800-387-7650

Written by: Amy Culliford
Translation by: Santiago Ochoa
Designed by: Rhea Wallace
Series Development: James Earley
Proofreader: Kathy Middleton
Educational Consultant: Christina Lemke M.Ed.
Photographs: Shutterstock: NPDstock: cover (tl); Menna: cover (tr); Laurinson Crusoe: cover (b); Amy K. Mitchell p. 1; Pete Pahham: p. 3, 14; Zane Vergara: p. 4, 14; Natelle: p. 7; Alexey Stiop: p. 9; FooTToo: p. 10-11; wk1003mike: p. 12; fotorauschen: p. 13

Published in Canada
Crabtree Publishing
616 Welland Ave.
St. Catharines, Ontario
L2M 5V6

Published in the United States
Crabtree Publishing
347 Fifth Avenue,
Suite 1402-145
New York, NY, 10016

Library and Archives Canada Cataloguing in Publication
Available at the Library and Archives Canada

Library of Congress Cataloging-in-Publication Data
Available at the Library of Congress

Paperback: 9781039624481
Ebook: 9781039625327
Epub: 9781039624900

Printed in the U.S.A./CP202510